Words of Inspiration:
THE LOVE COLLECTION II

By Robert T Sells

Words of Inspiration:
THE LOVE COLLECTION II

ROBERT T. SELLS
Author, Motivational Speaker, Award-winning Poet
and
Spoken Word Artist

Words of Inspiration:
THE LOVE COLLECTION II

Other Books in the Words of Inspiration Poetry Series

A Collection of Poems for
the One You Love

Speak Healing

ROBERT T. SELLS

Author, Motivational Speaker, Award-winning Poet &
Spoken Word Artist

EMAIL:
wordsofinspirationministries@gmail.com

WEBSITE:
www.wordsofinspirationministries.com

BLOG:
http://theanointedpoet.blogspot.com/

PERISCOPE:
www.periscope.tv/wordsofinmin

YOUTUBE:
www.youtube.com/theanointedpoet

ROBMAR PUBLISHING
Franklin, TN

Printed in the United States of America 2016

Words of Inspiration

Copyright © 2016 Robert T Sells

ISBN# 978-0-692-65024-0

I dedicate this book, first and foremost, to my Lord and Savior, Jesus Christ; it is because of You that I am alive today, and without you none of this would be possible. They are Your words that grace the pages of this book.

Secondly, I dedicate this book to my beautiful wife. Without you I would not be who I am today. I love you very much and always will pretty lady. Everything I do is because of you. Every day I live I pray to God that my love for you will continue to grow. I will love you forever.

Thirdly, I dedicate this book to my dad. He went home to be with the Lord on Good Friday, April 2010. I will never forget how much support he gave me when he first found out I was going to be an author. I love you dad and I always will. You have been a strong example to me of who a man should be and an ongoing inspiration for me to continue this work.

Acknowledgements

To my pastor, Pastor Kevin Jackson of New Wine
Ministries: thank you for all of your support and
spiritual guidance.

To my friend and mentor Dr. Princess Fumi
Hancock: thank you for your continued prayers and
wisdom for this journey.

Table of Contents

My Love

I love you uncontrollably
I love you beyond anything you can contain
I love you unconditionally
There's not enough room on the largest planet
That can contain the amount of love you will receive
from me

If I had twelve million lifetimes
To express to you how I feel
It would barely scratch the surface
Of the overwhelming feeling inside
When thought of you arise in me.

I love you endlessly

There's no finite point in time

That I can highlight and say

This is the end of my love for you

For my love for you is infinite

And like the rings on our fingers

It is without beginning or end

It just is... always!

Two Whole Years

It's hard to believe that two whole years have come
and gone

It seems it was just yesterday

That from two we became one

God parted the waters of time

He released the sun

Flowers showered on our days

Moonbeams on our nights

The Holy Spirit of God became our night light

As we celebrate our anniversary I know

There are miles and miles to go

But I thank God for the presence of you in my life

Because you make the miles seem like inches

My love for you just increases every year

My heart is filled to the brim as my love cinches

The soul of you my dear

As I think of you I hear God speak to me

"Forever you are to be together", God told me

"Let me work in your lives,

as you pay your tithes and trust Me

you'll begin to realize

that nothing will be impossible for you

Always be in agreement in everything you do

and you will do immeasurably more as two

than you would've ever done as one".

So let's heed the word of the Holy Spirit of God

Let's do what He tells us to do

And we will live in peace as one

As the anointed couple who love each other the way

God wanted us to do

Cause as we do every battle is already won.

The Woman for Me

Sitting here in my bedroom gentle thoughts of you
fill my head

Calm peonies fill my subconscious mind

Similes, no realities of the beauty I would've left
behind

Had it not been for God

Invasions of roses,

The tropical scent of love poses

A threat to the enemy's plans

No woman as wonderful as you should be with this
man

But God says different

For He presented you to me with no in kind blemish

A perfect fit and an answer to the premise

You are the one for me

You are destined to be

The other part of my unit

The perfect fit

Truly legit we were meant

To stand as one we love each other

The sun rises and falls on your beauty

I search no longer for another

For the Lamb of God has seen fit to bless me

With His most elegant creature on this earth

He shows me in you the best me

No rest for me, but lest he

Show me what my mission for us is it is useless to resist thee

Oh Lord I thank you

For sending me your angel

Because my sweetie you are everything I prayed for

The salt of my earth I delayed for

The anti-wishing on a shining star for

The completion of our union by far for

No woman can do for me what you do

No woman can seal it for me or renew

My spirit the way you do

No woman can intensify my love like you

I justify my love for you in everything I say and do

And I thank God for telling me who

You were in His timing and not mine

And I thank God for allowing me to love

The most incredible woman of my time

In Your Eyes

When I look in your eyes
  I see me in you
I see all the joy my heart feels
I see my mirror image
The way God meant it to be

When I look into your eyes
I see us walking down a long road
With no end
It trails off to anywhere
Nowhere, then everywhere
For that is wherever you are

When I look in your eyes
I see the renewal of love
I take my love back to the library
To have more time
Added to it
I'm inserting my ATM card
Into love's ATM
And I continue getting back more
And as I keep taking out
I see my balance climb

When I look in your eyes

A slight breeze continues

Through my mind

Blowing thoughts of forever love

To warm my heart

And every time I look again

It's full to overflowing

Warm to the touch

I get emotional now and then

When I look in your eyes

I see children, grandchildren

A house with a white picket fence

And a dog barking out back

And then suddenly it all makes sense

When I look in your eyes, I see...

...Forever

The Past 3 Years

As each passing day goes by
The impossible fades into non-existence
For with each new sunrise
Is a grace renewed
And another day I am blessed
To be spending with you

Every morning for the past three years
I got to wake up
And be greeted by the woman God put on this earth
For me as I take up
My cross and follow Jesus
I know you are at one with me
Like no other woman on this earth
Every evening I get to see
A smile that moves mountains
Eyes that outshine the stars
And beauty that overtakes the sun

Beauty as natural as a rose
Sprouting from between the thorns and thistles
Such as the way you sprouted up
In my life and drowned my worries and concerns

When you showed up
All my sad days became happy
When you showed up
All my darkness was replaced with sunshine
When you showed up
The will of God began for me
And there was nothing from that point on
That could stop it.

Sweetie you brought the sunshine to my life
For the past three years
You made my dark paths light
For the past three years
You wiped away all my tears with your love
And now I am so happy in my spirit
That I know that the past three years
Will be nothing compared to the rest of my life
For I have been united
With the most wonderful woman in the world
The woman who I am overjoyed to say is my wife.

Here and Now

I remember that first day
I sat there amazed
At what I was seeing
Angels sang an amorous lullaby
Into the spirit of my being
The wind whistled through the recesses of my mind
While a small pilot light lit in my heart
"I couldn't possibly be in love again"
I would say to myself
I never felt anything for this woman since the start

We sang on the praise team at church together
We spoke in passing, gave high fives,
Laughed and joked with each other
Who knew we were equally yoked
Who knew I would fall in love
After all I've been though in my life
Who knew that after all that pain I experienced
All the doubts that had developed
Over the years of being loved wrong
Who knew I would ever find another wife

God knew because He sent me you

And he told me what to do

At the proper time, at the proper place he told me to

Look at the woman He affectionately called "you"

As I turned to look He showed me you

Not the "you" I'd seen many times

But the "you" God knew

The "you" that was the only "you"

He knew would be the only "you"

Who was meant for me

I knew at that moment it was love

As I caught your passing gaze

My heart worked out a way

To convince me it wasn't a fleeting feeling

For God had showed me the rest of my days

With the most beautiful woman I've ever known

So I quickened my thoughts

Forward to the day

When I knew I would be your husband

Just one look propelled me through 13 dimensions

My love grew instantly

I felt sensations of love

Creations of forever danced in my heart

Palpitations drumming to the beat of always

And at that moment I knew

That I would confess my love for you

At that moment I knew

That I would be faithful in everything I do for you

Sweetheart you're all I need

You are the one with whom I'll be

So I dedicate my life to you

I profess my love for you

I can no longer be afraid to love

Because now my dreams have come true

I move forward in my commitment

And I thank God for a woman so sweet

I thank God for allowing me to see

The woman He destined for me to be with

So from this day forward I share my life with you

From this day forward I give my love to you

From this day forward I promise to love you

You are my wife from this day until forever I vow

To become your husband and your one true love...

...Here and Now

Timeless

Timeless is the beauty which makes up you
To your piercing eyes there is no end
No way to surmise
The state you leave my mind in its no surprise

That time stands still
The seconds count to nil
And all efforts to try to exert my own will
Are futile
For all the while I'm stoned
By the energy of your smile
And time stands still
Just like the effects of a sleeping pill
You knock me out
As my mind emits a high pitch shrill

And I know I'm stuck in time
In a romantic twilight zone whirlwind with no end
My verbal sounds are like a mime
Void and none
I am drunk on love
Straight from God above through you
And I stay this way, everyday

Then my mind finally allows me to speak

And after the silence I emit a whisper as I can only say...

...Timeless

An Anointed Wife

If I could take all the love from the world
And put it in one woman
She would be you
For you are someone who's heart
I knew from the start
That I wanted to be the one man
Who said you were set apart
To become for me
What God intended you to do
And from that point forward I knew
I would live my life with you

It was as if God parted the saints
Whispered in my ear to turn my head
To see what is not what ain't
And as I saw you God began to paint
A picture of you and I
And me singing you a lullaby
And singing praises to the Lord
For it is He, not I, who saw
You with me and then my cold heart began to thaw
And once again would feel love
As that directly from our Father above

So then I'd work up the nerve

To stay straight and not swerve

To ask you out and hear you say no

And I would hear God say "Don't go my son

You don't know what I know"

So I stayed around and watched

As you and I clowned on the phone I could see

Finally that you were meant for me

And as I promised God I'd live my life

For Him and be thankful to Him

For this day He showed me

The woman He had made my wife

My Kind of Girl

I know that what I feel is real
So why would I think of trying to conceal
The very thing God promised to me
When I was eating a spiritual meal
Of the Word of God on my life to be

I knew at that moment we were meant to be
I knew right away without trying to see
The future with my natural eye
For when I knew I blinded my eye
To the things I can see
And opened my eye
To the things of God
And upon saying goodbye to the world
It allowed God to introduce me
To the woman I would call
"My kind of girl".

When "I" Becomes "We"

There's no telling how many things had to happen in our lives

To get us to this day

So many decisions that had to be made

So many times to go through while we were sad

So many appointments missed

So many people we dissed

So many places lived in

So many times we'd give in

So many tears we cried

So many reconciliations we tried

But finally after so much heartache

After so many things gone wrong

We are now at a time

When we are led by the Lord

And now God has us in a place

Where together we will bask in the glory of His face

And then there will be no trace

Of our rugged past

Because our past lives, past roads we've taken

Have led us to each other at last

And now we can rest and be sure

Of what God has in store for us together

We must operate with a knowing that God is our Lord

And he will bless us together forever

So from this day forward I promise you

If you take my hand and go with me

We will be led by God to the ultimate union of our marriage

When God causes the "I" for both of us to become "we".

My Angel

I know God sent me an angel
It shows in everything you do
You are so in tune with my every need
That I just have to thank God for you

I know God sent me an angel
It shows in the things you say
Your voice just heals and delivers me so easily
That I eagerly await our wedding day

I know God sent me an angel
It shows in the way you are
Your very ways my "Mighty Woman of God"
Are better for me than others by far

I know God sent me an angel
It shows in the way you love me
For the first time in my life I know I'm loved
And I know that from my past I've been set free

I know God sent me an angel
It shows in the way you look
Because the beauty you show me everyday
Cannot be learned from a book

I know God sent me an angel

Because He speaks to me every day about you

And God reminds me every day how happy I'll be

From the moment I say "I Do"

Destined Love

In all my life I've never met
A woman as wonderful as you
We've had our ups, we've had our downs
But in all that we made it through

Every time I think about
How beautiful you are in every way
A chill runs down my spine when I think
How we almost didn't make it to this day

Then through it all you bore a child
A son who become the priority in my life
A son who was born through one act of love
From the woman who thankfully became my wife

I didn't know while we were apart
How important the years were that we were together
During those two years we built a foundation in God
That would last no matter the weather

Now today we are happily married
And already making our house a home
Now today I just want to let you know
That from a love like yours I will never roam

Finally sweetie I just want you to know
I thank God for the day we first met
I will truly love you forever my dear wife
And from this day on our future is set

Proverbs 31 Woman

God decided one day he would make
A woman like no other.
One who would worship and serve Him daily
Like a child served by his mother.

In this woman he put all things
He wanted to represent Him
Every fruit of the Spirit including love,
The most important and by far not just a whim.

He made this woman to be just like Himself,
Wonderful and always pleasing to His eyes
And He knew who He had in store for her
Her eternal husband who would be her prize.

Once this woman was presented to the man
Who God destined to be her husband
He let her go to be the woman He knew she was
And then on Aug 13, 2005 he took her hand.

Yes my dear the man is me, the woman is you

You are the most important person in my life

And I will always thank God for the Proverbs 31 woman

That He created just to be my wife.

Everyday Love

Those men who don't know what true love is
Haven't been blessed enough to meet you
And they have yet to discover
What a true woman of God can do

Sweetie you've touched my heart in so many ways
It seems you sometimes know what I want before I ask
Making wonderful my every day
And making light my every task

Every day I thank God for you
Because for me there is no greater woman on earth
You make every day better and better for me
And you increase my spiritual self-worth.

With God I know all things are possible
There is nothing I won't be able to accomplish or do
Add you to the mix and we become an unbeatable force for God
For together we are stronger than one plus one equals two

I thank God because He knew you were made for me

Even before I arrived on this planet

He formed you from me before the beginning of time

And established our union of love before we even said it.

I know we were meant to be together sweetheart

Because the Holy Spirit told me so

And my love for you will grow more and more each day

As I continue to get closer to you than the day before.

Empty

As I sit in eager expectation of the next time you hold my hand

I begin to draw my proverbial line in the sand

And count the seconds as they slowly grind to a psychological halt

In the romantic time clock in my mind

An hourglass slowly seeping with salt

That never seems to empty

Empty?

Empty is the next time we touch or make contact

Empty is the next time I experience your incredible presence

The way you just have an inevitable knack

Of washing me away with the bubbles of your effervescence

And before I know it I'm floating again

I take a breathalyzer and flunk again

I am under arrest for loving without reason again

And then we part to go throughout our day

Empty becomes full all over again

And I watch and watch the salts of time

Eager to know why each grain isn't trying

To pass on through that small opening because I

Grow tired of waiting for empty to come by

Tired of knowing that empty will be my blessing

Because my woman of God will touch me a

And cause me to begin regressing

To the day of our first date as I was working on impressing

You because I knew you would be my wife

You were refreshing because

You knew then and now the things that I want

And during the empty you move me in ways

That only God knows I need every day

Leaving me wanting to experience more and more

Of you and praying for "full" to move farther away than before

Because it is during the empty that I find romance

It is during the empty that my heart can dance

It is during the empty that my voice sings at last

This is love this is love

And it is from God for sure

And because it is from God that I praise Him forever

And I thank him forever

For the empty in the hourglass with you

That He has made to last.

Unconditional Love

They met at Starbucks one day
    They probably never thought
Life would carry them this way
They fell in love and made their plans
To marry each other
To become one together
To live as husband and wife forever

Who could've seen this coming?
The day that changed their life
The day that tragedy would befall
The woman who was going to become his wife
Just one accident changed the course
Of their well-planned and thought-out life

One life-changing accident
Caused his true love
To slip into a coma
Battling death every day silently
So she could remain on this earth
To live among us
As she fought for her life
Her family was there

Praying and remaining by her side
But one thing I didn't expect
The man who was going to be her husband
Was doing something we do not normally see

He stayed there with her and the family
Helping to nurse her back to health
Dealing with her sudden inadequacies
And the numerous challenges she faced
Without a promise of future wealth
This man was very young
He had his whole life ahead of him
He could've moved on to greener pastures
And took up with another woman
Who could meet his every selfish need
From this day to every one after
He could've moved on
And enjoy the rest of his life
Without having to feed or clean
Push around or carry
The woman he would call his wife

But alas this was meant to be

This man didn't want to find anyone else

Because he knew where his heart was

He didn't need to marry anyone else

To fulfill what would've been an empty life

Because in his mind and heart

He had all he needed

In this beautiful woman he'd met

And he knew it from the start

"How could he leave her now?" he said

As he captured all those watching

With his sincerest, loving glare

"When she needed me most,

How could I leave the woman that I love,

When she really needed me to be there?"

So as I watched this man profess his love

For this woman who means so much

A prayer came to my mind

"Lord if anyone deserves your grace it's them

So please heal her miraculously

Touch her with your healing hands

And stir up your Spirit in her voraciously

Let her rise from her fallen state

By a simple touch from you Lord

And let her be joined in marriage

To this special man who loves her

More than any man ever will or could.

Love

Love
It goes beyond infatuation

Which usually happens

The moment you experience

The physical attraction

Fake happiness starts and ends

With a simple teasing

That immediately sets

Our feelings in motion

Love

It goes beyond sex

Which usually happens

Too quickly for you to realize

That all it was

Was the person

You decided to sin with

Sex gets in the way

Then you realize

True love

was never there to begin with

It was at that "moment"

That you realized

That you idolized
A "moment"

Love
Starts where infatuation ends
It has no prior requirements
No physical appearance
No heated intimate act
Can top a true love desire

Love
Causes a man
To say "no" to another woman
So he can say "yes" constantly
To the "only woman"
Who he wants to miss
It's the woman
God has for him
He loves her unconditionally
And he seals it with a ring
And with a kiss

Love

Causes a woman

To say "no" to temporal pleasure

Or a "fake" passionate kiss

She ignores the seemingly "forever" advances

Which turn out to be "just for now" moments

In order to have eternal bliss

Love

Causes someone to love

The person, not the image

It never fails at what it does

It never lets you down

It never comes around

Only for a moment

But forever.

Because You Loved Me

Because you loved me I
Loved you too at least I thought
I did everything I could
To take care of you
Went to work
Brought a check home for you
But all the while
I ignored the sign that said,
"Beware of you"
If I didn't do what I'm supposed to do

I didn't see what the problem was
I got up every day and went to work
And never missed, I was never late
I brought in big money I took care of you
I even let you clean the house
Wash my clothes and cook for me
While I yelled at you
"Watch the house while I go out
And hang with my friends"
I'd pick up women that didn't mind pleasing me
And didn't care where it would end
Isn't that what you wanted me to do?

And every once in a while

When you're weren't acting like I wanted you to

I'd take a flare to you

I'd slap you once or twice

Just to put a scare in you

I knock you down sometimes

Kick you and step on you

Because of me you'd go out of the house

With so much makeup

You look like a mime

But that's only because

You asked me one more time

Why haven't I married you?

Well I did

 So what more do you want from me?

Everything I did for you

I did because you loved me

But one day I got a hold of

That book they call the Bible

And I began to see everything I wasn't doing I

Began to see myself as the me I always said I
wouldn't be I

Saw I had gone down the wrong road too many times
I

Saw that the "I Love you's" I was saying I really
didn't mean I

Saw that what I was doing to you was what I thought
was right I

Thought it was right because I loved you

As I read the Bible I saw that

I really didn't love you like you loved me

I read how Jesus came to this earth

And died for you and me

And then I saw where it says

As men we should love our wives

As Christ loved the church unconditionally

Well He loved the church enough to die

For people he didn't know he gave His life

So that we can be free.

I now know what I didn't do

A tear came to my eye as I realized

I never died for you

Even though you loved me

I didn't love you
I didn't even know how to love me

I couldn't trust you
Because I couldn't even trust me
I couldn't be your best friend
Because I wasn't even a friend to me
I couldn't even hold you in my arms
And offer you shelter from the rain
Protect you from the flaming arrows
That the devil shot at you again and again
Because I didn't allow God to hold me

You see I learned that I wasn't ready to marry you
I learned that even though I thought I loved you
I wasn't trying to please you
Even though you cared for me
My spirit wasn't at ease with you
Oh God what have I done to you?
Jesus!!!!!!!!!!!!!!!!!!

Lord I want to be just like you
So I can love me then her
Lord I want to become just like you
So I can show her the "me" you intended for me to be
So you can love me and I can learn how to love you

Jesus as I become more like you

I can become the right kind of me

So I can love my wife

I want to become like Jesus

So I can love you as "my church" eternally

I want to become the Shepard to you my flock

I want to become Abraham to my Sarah

So I can hear you when you knock

On my door and I will open it

To let you in Jesus

And I will become you

And I will marry my wife

And she will become my church

I will become all things to all people

So I can learn how to nurture

And only then will I be able to love you dearly

When I become like Jesus I will always

Want you near me

I will protect you from all harm

I will pray for you and with you every day

I will read the word to you

And hold you in my arms at night

I will never let you go a day

Without knowing you are loved right

I will be the man of God you need me to be

I will lead this family like it's supposed to be

Led I will take care of your every

Spiritual, emotional, and physical need

I will love you until the end of eternity

I will lift you on a platform

Where no one else can touch you but God and me

And I will reside in this house with you forever

Baby I am a changed man now

I've become like Jesus

And as I lay this flower on your casket

I promise to love you forever

As you have loved me

I will never let you go again

And I now understand what it means to love

And it's all "because you first loved me".

Love... Applied

Love, applied to you
Is immeasurably enhanced
It becomes more than a feeling
More than "I already danced"

Love, applied to you
Goes beyond the ordinary emotion
It covers during the rain
Protects during trials
Supports during the down
And clears away the commotion

Love, applied to you
Is freedom
Love, applied to you
Is forever

One Moment

Yesterday I thought of you
And a warm feeling
Passed through me
As I thought of you
I realized
The warmth I felt was you

Yesterday I thought of you
It was only for one moment
A beautiful moment
That lasted just long enough
To comfort me
I knew type of love
Wasn't done yet

Yesterday I thought of you

And yes it was for one moment

Just one moment in time

Just one 24-hour moment

That blessed my soul

It was one 24-hour moment

That has lasted a lifetime

One Flesh

Before I was married
I wanted to know
What it would be like
To share a love so deep
That it often feels like
We're the same person
I wanted my marriage
To go beyond two people
Who love each other
But to transcend the "two"
And become "one"
Where my every thought
Is known before I think it
Where our very words
Are in agreement
Without even saying it

Before I was married
I wanted to know
What it would be like
To see the world
The way my spouse sees it
Before I shout and yell
About the way I see it

I wanted to know
How it felt
To pray together
To read the Bible together
To attend church
Without having to fight about it

Before I was married
I had so many ideas
Of what it would mean
To be one with someone
So wonderful and great
And now that I am
I see why God wanted me to wait
Because everything
I was shown by God
Is in you my love
In every possible way
And because of this
I'm grateful to know
That you and I will be "one flesh"
Forever and a day

The Wife Speaks (a poem from Marlas)

My Love is True

Each day I give to you a love so true because
Only God knew that you would be the one to

Rescue my heart from its dungeon of despair

That held me bound by the hurts and fears of

A past filled with no love and mountains of distrust

From the lifetime of misery and pain I had lived

Each day I give to you a love so true because

Only God knew that you would tear down the walls
the enemy built

Leaving me free to live again... free to live again!

I'm alive now and it's because of you

Loving me in ways that I never knew existed because
of the scabs

That covered me and the open wounds that leaked
with my blood

Essentially zapping the life from me

Each day I give to you a love so true because

Only God knew that your unconditional love would
bring me through

My eyes opened wide again

My heart began to sing again

My future looked bright again

I began to dance again...

To the song, our song of love and then
I loved without the reason... again!

Each day I give to you a love so true because
Only God knew what your love would do!

© Marlas J. Sells

A Word From the Author

The most beautiful aspect of having a relationship with God is knowing that He wants to have a relationship with us. While reading this book, you may have said to yourself, "I'd like to have a relationship with God." Or maybe at one point you were in close relationship with God but, for whatever reason, you backed away. God loves us so much that it doesn't matter what we've done, He still wants to be a part of our lives. Whether you want to ask God to come into your life for the first time or you are hearing the Holy Spirit calling you back into relationship with Him, it can be yours today. The Bible tells us that "... if you confess with your mouth the Lord Jesus and believe in your heart that God raised him from the dead, you will be saved." (Romans 10:9)

Simply pray this prayer with us:

Father God, forgive me for all of my sins. I believe that Jesus is your Son, that He died for my sins, that You raised Him from the dead and that He is now seated at your right hand. Jesus, I invite you to become Lord of my life, to rule and reign in my heart from this day forward. Father God, send your Holy Spirit to help me to obey and to do your will for my life. Jesus, thank you for loving me so much that you sacrificed your life for mine. Because you did, I now have eternal life. Lord Jesus, thank you for saving me. Amen.

If you prayed this prayer from your heart, you are now saved. Welcome to the family of God. We encourage you to find a local church where you can be baptized and grow in the knowledge of God through His Word. Begin to read the Bible daily and ask God to reveal His purpose for your life to you. We'd like to hear from you! Any questions, comments, concerns; or if you'd just like to share a thought with us, please send an email to:

wordsofinspirationministries@gmail.com.

God bless you, dear friend.

www.ingramcontent.com/pod-product-compliance
Lightning Source LLC
Chambersburg PA
CBHW071009040426
42443CB00007B/729